# Tantric Sex

## Introduction Handbook To Tantra

## By: More Sex More Fun Book Club

Hey,

Thank you very much for choosing this book!

Before we begin...

If you are interested in non-fiction sex books, head over to our partner site alexandramorris.com

Alexandramorris.com is a great site in the making. They publish e-books, paperbacks, audiobooks and blog posts written by up-and-coming writers and great freelancers. They also give away TONS of Audible coupon codes, Amazon gift cards, pdf copies of books totally free!

We really hope this books will give you valuable information to take your sex life to the next level. Enjoy and please leave an honest review after finishing it.

Best regards

losses, direct or indirect, which are incurred as a result of the use of information contained within this document, including, but not limited to, —errors, omissions, or inaccuracies.

# Table of Contents

# Introduction

The meaning of 'tantra' conjures up a myriad range of teachings, philosophies, and meanings and there will always be a huge debate when people discuss this rather esoteric topic. There will be people agreeing with some aspects of what you see and there will be people disagreeing with you strongly. Yet, you must know that the actual term 'tantra' signifies something very meaningful.

To understand the meaning of this word, we would have to start with another Indian word called 'sutra.' Sutras were critical texts of Hinduism, Jainism, and Buddhism. The sutra that gained maximum fame in the Western World is, perhaps, the Kama Sutra which is a text that talks in detail about erotic and sexual arts. By the way, this sutra is in no way connected to Tantra. Another equally famous sutra is that of Patanjali called the Yoga Sutra.

Let us start again with the word, sutra, whose literal meaning is 'thread' and refers to a particular thread or line of thought. Some believe that this 'thread' refers to the physical threads that bind the text together.

So, the sutra is a single thread of thought and tantra is an entire system of thought. The Sanskrit meaning of 'tantra' is 'loom.' We are not just talking about the cloth that is woven with the threads, but the entire machinery on which the piece of cloth is made. Originally, sutras came in the form of books, whereas tantras were taught by the guru or teacher directly to his disciples or students. Soon, considering the highly literate society that this part of society was, the oral

1

teachings also took the form of books, notes, summaries, etc.

Now, let us come to the 6<sup>th</sup> century in Europe. During this time, the Roman Empire was in tatters and there was absolutely no stability leading to the increased growth of warfare and petty battles amongst smaller warlords. The worst affected aspects of society were education and knowledge which had reached abysmal depths and illiteracy and ignorance was rampant in Europe.

The Eastern society, particularly India, was on a path of stability and growth. Education and intellectual thinking were on the rise in this entire nation. Kashmir, specifically became a melting pot of cultures and yet, ancient worship rituals and traditions still existed here; especially the worship of Siva and Shakti; more on this in the next chapter.

Here, the word 'tantra' or loom has been given another connotation; that of weaving together Siva, the representative of consciousness, with Shakti, the representative of power. Also, the loom could be the weaving together of Siva, Shakti, and other 'sutras' or threads of Vedic tradition and culture. At this time in the Kashmir valley, Jainism and Buddhism were also thriving and some aspects of those religions always began to be woven together to combine Siva and Shakti to create a new form of thought or 'Tantra.'

This is just the beginning of Tantra. Read on for more.

# Chapter One: History and Origins of Tantra

Now, that you know the basic etymology of 'sutra' and 'Tantra' let us dive right in and get more information as to the origins and the history of this rather misunderstood and misinterpreted system of thought. Tantra can be believed to be the weaving of the 'sutras' of Siva and that of Shakti to achieve the divine and transcend beyond human senses.

There were multiple oral traditions that were imbibed into the Tantra of weaving together of Siva and Shakti. These traditions were most likely derived from Dravidian matriarchal societies that honored and respected the female aspect of life. In these traditions, women were very powerful influencers and great teachers too.

There were highly powerful and meaningful rituals to mark transition points. These rituals were all centered upon nature and were very important connecting lines to nature. Most importantly, these female-oriented traditions rarely separated these rituals from routine life. They did not have priestly class or any kind of monastic order which controlled the other parts of the society or tradition.

These teachings or the Tantra thoughts found a lot of popularity among the burgeoning middle class in India, which was becoming wealthier and more powerful than before the time we are talking about (around the 6th century). This emerging middle class was more or less unaffected by the caste-consciousness of the Vedic nature and also by the monastic male-dominated Buddhist philosophy of the times.

3

Additionally, these shamanic-like traditions taught that enlightenment was possible right here, right now. These traditions were practical and easy to follow unlike the scholarly and monastic teachings of the conventional religions in force at that time. These traditions were very immediate and very vibrant too.

The immediacy of the outcomes was very attractive as people did not have the compulsion to wait for reincarnations and rebirths for salvation. Divinity was not described in any abstract and distant form consisting of a collection of confusing deities. On the other hand, divinity was explained as something that is all-pervasive and that which each of us is a part of. In fact, divinity is not something that we are a part of, but it was the whole of the Universe.

Nothingness, as described in Buddhism, this was not an easy concept to understand for the average person. The concept of nothingness was changed into a form that was easier to interpret and comprehend; that nothingness became an all-pervading, omnipresent, and universal consciousness.

The physical world which was considered a deception to the traditional view became an illusion in this middle-class accepted new tradition. Everything and everyone in this universe became a differently projected part of the universal consciousness. As we get better at understanding, the awareness of the non-duality concept, we slowly began to understand the illusionary aspect of what our five senses project to us until finally, we can now visualize and accept the entire Universe including us, the world around us, and the Divine, as one and the same.

All these teachings together were referred to as Tantra and continued through the entire Classical Era, which lasted for about 400-500 years. Multiple individual and independent teachers created many lineages that had among them a few diversities but mostly commonalities.

Kashmir Shaivism was one such lineage created and remained highly prevalent for a few centuries. However, the Tantra lineage highly influenced both the then prevalent Hinduism and Buddhism. The Hinduism as we know it today is particularly influenced by the Tantra tradition. Buddhism created an entirely new sub-sect called Vajrayana Buddhism that still survives in the Himalayas even today.

Therefore, Tantra was viewed as a spiritual science by many independent practitioners. They believed this science was available for adaptation to one's set of beliefs. It is free of any one particular religious dogma or principles and instead, drew commonalities from all.

Irrespective of who created a particular Tantra sub-sect (for want of a better word), the following commonalities were found across these different types:

- Direct relationship between the gurus (teachers) to the disciples (students)
- Mindfulness in all aspects
- Rituals were used to increase awareness
- All arbitrary rules of culture and religion were rejected
- Acceptance of followers irrespective of caste, gender, nationality, language, etc.
- Unmitigated access to participating in the rituals connecting to the divine

- Belief in the body sensations including sexual experiences as a path that will lead to the divine; it is important not to replace this path of sensual pleasures to reach the divine as a distraction

While sexuality and sensuality are debated on their importance by people from different belief systems, the fact that sexual experiences are part and parcel of the means of achieving the divine in Tantra philosophy is irrefutable. While some manuals choose the union of male and female energies through the sexual practice to attempt to meet the divine energy, there are other cases in evidence wherein tantra practitioners including established gurus of those times were imprisoned and branded for using licentious behavior to corrupt the priestly Brahmin class.

While the extant texts are not very vocal on the points of sexual union and sexual pleasure, there is no doubt that the texts were written by highly learned scholars of those times who were well-versed and practiced in the Tantric systems and rituals. Additionally, many of these scholars chose to keep the secrets of direct transmission of energy highly 'secretive' as it was ordered by their own teachers to do so. What happened behind the 'veils' can only be surmised and speculated and not really known except by the ones who had achieved the capability to know and experience the outcome of the direct transmission.

## Art and Architecture

While the texts remain inconclusive about the use of sexual practices, the art and architecture that exist even today are highly illustrative and leave no doubt in the minds of the modern man to the use of sex in Tantra philosophy. The sculptors and temple architecture are replete with vivid and potent imagery of the union of female (yoni) with the male (lingam) genitals through the act of sex.

The female yoni consists of the vulva and the vagina and the male lingam is representative of the penis. The imagery of the male and female deities are shown locked in carnal embraces. Most of the tantra illustrations present the consort and the practitioner in sexual union pose. Here it is important to note that the male is usually taken to be the practitioner and the female is the consort. However, in truth, Tantra philosophy treats both equally and both could be practitioners and consorts in turn. Many of the great teachers were women while many of the writers of texts were male.

## Disappearance of Tantra

The classical form of tantra more or less disappeared around the 1100s when Islam took its roots in India. Buddhism almost completely disappeared and tantric rituals and practices were also mostly forgotten. Yet, three forms of Tantra continued to survive and does even to this day and the three forms include:

1. Hatha Yoga – this lineage of Tantra retains and preserves the practical rituals and teachings including and, specifically, the embodiment of mindfulness practices; however without much philosophical depth
2. Vajrayana Buddhism – retained the original rituals and texts along with the philosophical teachings around Buddhism
3. The Sri Vidya lineage through Brahmanism – this lineage completing removed and cleared all the

rule-rejecting aspects of tantra and became sanitized under the approval of Brahmanism and Vedic context

## Tantra in the Contemporary Age

The largely forgotten Tantra philosophy came to the fore again nearly 800-900 years later in Europe. This rediscovered format is replete with the original vibrancy and diversity that existed during its primary days around the $5^{th}$ century. The reason for this comeback is easy to understand, and here's why and how it happened:

Even before connecting with India, Nepal, and other Eastern cultures, European spirituality already had an element of secret sexual traditions that were considered sacred. When the minds of these eastern and western secret sex-based philosophies met, the resurgence of tantra happened. The modern tantra came alive combining elements of the classical tantric texts of India along with the western sexual mysticism creating a new kind of amalgamated, reconstituted, and reformulated thought. The contemporary tantra system incorporates the elements of breathing techniques, energy flow, and mindfulness to bring alive the spirit of the passionate divine. And thus, Tantra was reborn in its present avatar.

Even today, some teachers and schools are aligned to the Kashmir Shaivism lineage and teach and propagate rituals and teachings from this school. Many others are promoting Vajrayana Buddhism that is simplified and made more adaptable in the Western way of life. Even teachers and followers of the Sri Vidya lineage are rediscovering and reconnecting with the sexual dimensions of their tantra and are redesigning concepts to include these elements as well.

Osho or Bhagwan Shree Rajneesh founded a Tantra school of thought based on his own understanding and interpretations of the tantric systems. In fact, his teachings reached far and wide across the globe and gave rise to a new word called, 'neotantra.' David Deida also used tantric principles initially to set up his own teaching school.

Many of the contemporary teachings use the performance of sex as the center for achieving divinity and it plays a very important role and forms the foundations of the modern tantric schools. Yet others do reject 'sexuality' completely from their teachings. Again, if you removed the sexual aspect and prominence of the sexual act from these contemporary tantric teachings, you will find the same common threads that we found when we studied diverging tantra schools that opened in the 5th century in India. These commonalities include:

- Personal and enlightened transmissions directly from teacher to student; it is important (just like old times) to have a spiritually gifted teacher
- Practice of mindfulness
- The importance of ritual
- Open to all irrespective of caste, creed, race, gender, language, nationality, etc.
- Teachings that promise direct access to the divine and related experiences

**More in the Western Form of Tantra**

There are four forms of tantra that are popular in the Western world today and they include:

**White Tantra** – This is an esoteric form of tantra practiced using sexual energy as the foundation while leveraging on the power of meditation, visualization, and control of breath to seek divine enlightenment. This is usually practiced alone by an individual.

**Red Tantra** – This includes the principles of White Tantra along with using sexual techniques on and with another partner in play

**Pink Tantra** – This is the most popular tantra system that is in use in the West and includes the principles, rituals, and practices of the White and the Red Tantra. It is focused on relationships between couples and uses devotional energy through the heart for solving relationship problems and issues.

**Black Tantra** – Almost out of favor today, this format employs sexual energies to change things in people outside of the practitioners and usually comes with an intention to harm others.

## Role of Women in Tantra

In tantric traditions, a woman has been accorded as having a higher spiritual attitude than a man driven by a higher intensity in the following elements as compared to a man:

- Her frame
- Her emotions
- Her psychic evolution

Therefore, as per tantric traditions, it is believed that achieving enlightenment through the awakening of the Kundalini Shakti is easier in a woman's body than a man's. Another reason for this belief is the idea that when a man achieves a higher plane of consciousness and comes back to this plane after that experience, he is not able to bring back some of those experiences to this realm whereas a woman can do this.

When a man goes deep into his consciousness and then returns to gross awareness, a kind of a veil seems to fall in between the two planes for him. However, for a woman, this veil does not fall leaving the experiences from the higher consciousness to be brought into the gross consciousness.

Additionally, a woman's state of awareness is spiritually charged and this charge is reflected even in the gross life in the form of that tender look, feelings of sympathy and understanding for others' pains, etc. In fact, many tantric practitioners are of the opinion that in the absence of women, this world will become a desert with nothing but the stark surroundings; no color, no love, no passion, etc.

In Kundalini yoga, the mooladhara chakra in a man is located in a very congested area with little or no physical access. On the other hand, the mooladhara chakra of a woman is easily accessible and even be touched and activated easily. This makes it very easy for the awakening of the spirits in a woman's body than a man's which is why the woman is often given a higher spiritual place than a man in tantric systems.

The woman has always been the energy transporter whereas the man has always been the medium. This woman who helps in transportation a man's energy need not be a wife only. She could be a daughter, a disciple, or a mother. Mary was the mother of Jesus Christ whereas the Mother in the Aurobindo Ashram was a disciple.

Tantric traditions worship the woman as a goddess. There are 64 yoginis, who are the female gender of yogis. Shakti is the creator and Siva is the instrument. Without Shakti, Siva cannot create and in all Tantric systems, this belief of the union of man and woman needed for evolution and progress is many times misinterpreted as mere sexual pleasure.

In summary, from an Eastern viewpoint, Tantra is not relegated to getting heightened sexual pleasure or finding an improved way of having sex but is a way of life in which you use everyday experiences of the world (including sex) and convert them into divine experiences. Tantra teaches that you do not need to withdraw from worldly things to achieve divine enlightenment, but if you focus your energies mindfully on the routine day-to-day activities of life, you can get divine enlightenment because everything in this universe is part of the divine.

In the Western world, sadly, Tantra has been relegated to a practice that consists of esoteric sex out of the reach of people who don't understand it. In fact, there are multiple schools that market Tantra sex as a solution for sexual dysfunctions and problems ranging from boredom to other severe issues. Well, Tantra is more than this. It is a way of life and incorporating the practices consistently will help you lead a more fulfilled and understanding life than before.

All spiritual paths are always undertaken along with a woman for company. Similarly, a woman cannot undertake a spiritual path successfully without a man and so the equality of man and woman comes into play. One cannot survive without the other. In fact, there is a famous portrait of Shiva that is represented as one-half male and the other half as female which is what Tantra is all about; the combining of the female and male energies to achieve divine enlightenment.

# Chapter Two: Benefits of Following Tantra Practices

While there is a common misconception in the Western world about Tantra being only a system to increase sexual pleasure, the previous chapter, I hope, has helped you understand that this wonderful system goes beyond mere sexuality. This chapter is, therefore, dedicated to giving you the benefits of practicing tantric traditions. There are multiple elements in Tantra teachings that in the growth and development of an individual spiritual journey and his or her physical health. Let's look at some of them.

Before we go there, there is one more word of caution. The tantric texts are written in a difficult language using codes and formats that are not easy for an average person to read and interpret correctly. It is precisely for this reason that there are so many fraudulent schools spreading the wrong kind of information about this ancient and valuable belief system. The first thing to do is to become associated with a school that is authentic and reputable so that you can get all the benefits of a direct guru-disciple relationship.

Tantra is actually a system to help you achieve a higher plane of consciousness, referred to as Samadhi. The use of sex is only an instrument to achieve this Samadhi state. The actual act of sex is designed to take you beyond carnal pleasures that are limited to human senses. While the pleasure aspect of sex is also heightened through the use of tantric practices, these practices are also helpful in improving your physical and spiritual health.

There are usually two paths of Tantric practices that are used; the left-hand path and the right-hand path. For the average person, the left-hand path is considered most appropriate as it helps in achieving tantric enlightenment without sacrificing sexual pleasure. The right-hand path is more for the highly advanced practitioner and may not suit the needs of the average beginner. The processes in the right-hand path focus on intense meditative and symbolic techniques connected to sexual energy but without participating in the actual sexual act itself. Both these paths are 'correct' and it is not possible to say which is better than the other.

Tantra principles are based on a presumption that sexual energy comes from the base chakras including:

- Mooladhara chakra
- Svadhisthana chakra
- Manipura chakra

All the above chakras are located either at the navel level or below it. This sexual energy originating from the base chakras can be moved up to the upper chakras which are:

- Anahata or the heart chakra
- Visuddha or the throat chakra
- Anja or the third eye chakra
- Sahasrara or the crown chakra

The deliberate movement of the sexual energy from the base chakras to the upper chakras through tantric practices and rituals is designed to enhance both sexual and spiritual experience for the practitioners. The benefits include more fulfilling and more sustaining outcomes of both the sexual and spiritual experiences than before.

The tantric practices not only gives enhanced and the ultimate sexual pleasure that all of us strive to achieve but also benefits our physical and spiritual growth. The tantric practices, if done correctly and as per set norms, will help in producing sensations of bliss through love and sexual union from the human perspective and also from the perspective of joining the male and female energies through the act.

In the commonly practiced sexual encounters, most of the participants voice a sense of dissatisfaction and incompletion from the act in addition to feeling exhausted after reaching sexual peaks. This rather debilitating feeling of exhaustion is not just temporary but can easily spill over into other aspects of your emotional and physical life leaving you tired and fatigued more often than you'd like.

The loss of life energy or prana is bound to lead to health imbalances that can ultimately lead you to not enjoy the act at all. Using a few asanas, yoga postures, and some techniques from the teachings of Tantra, it is possible for a couple to preserve sexual energy and direct it upwards making sure every cell in the body is awakened through these practices.

For example, there is a technique referred to as transfiguration in tantra in which a couple sit in front of each other (fully clothed) without any physical contact and gaze into each other's eyes. It is important not to reduce this technique to a mere staring exercise. This tantric exercise requires you to be with your partner in a very intimate and profound way. By following this practice diligently, you will notice that there will come a time when both of you can see a personality beyond the eyes.

Each of you will see a certain beauty in the other that is impossible to ignore, reject or hate. Finding this almost pure enigma in each other will create a kind of love in the relationship that will go beyond human expectations and requirements from the each other allowing for free love to flow between the partners resulting in a deeper and more connected relationship.

Here are some of the physical benefits reported by practitioners of Tantra-based techniques driven by increased and seamless energy flow through the bloodstream into every nook and corner of the body:

- Improved toning of muscles
- Rejuvenated and revitalized skin texture leading to improved complexion
- Reduced movement of the spinal cord and slow back pain
- Reduction in fat deposits
- Release of toxins from the body
- Maintenance of youthful energy and looks along with improved physical vitality
- Reduction in wrinkles
- Firmer breasts
- Toning of muscles in the hip and the abdomen resulting in a flatter tummy and improved gait quality
- Calf muscles were highly regenerated
- A sustained sense of joy and happiness
- Reduction in menstrual secretions along with reduced premenstrual symptoms

Men practitioners also reported increased benefits from the preservation and redirection of sexual energy resulting in a healthier body and improved creative energy flow throughout the system. Tantra practices encourage the consumption of a low-protein macrobiotic diet that has a balanced amount of yin and yang to match the feminine and masculine balance resulting from following tantric practices.

Women practitioners are highly benefited as well as Tantra practices help in building and improving overall general health by channelizing the preserved energy right through the body. Tantra techniques help to calm the body and mind while improving energy levels. Practicing tantra techniques is a way for people to retreat themselves from this mad, hectic world and re-energize their body and mind. Especially, through the regular practice of Tantra yoga asanas which call for steady and slow movements of the body moving from one asana to another seamlessly. The conscious breathing done during this time is always a method to calm down your mind.

## More Benefits of Practicing Tantra

In addition to the general benefits mentioned above, tantra yoga is known to benefit by helping people deal with the following conditions by taking advantage of increased energy levels in the body:

- Stiffness in the body
- Stress and anxiety
- General fatigue
- Shoulder and back problems

While enlightenment may not happen overnight by Tantra practices (as it is not some kind of flashy miracle operation), sustained efforts at getting the right techniques and performing them patiently will go a long way in improving your spiritual and physical well-being. Of course, a healthy body is a prerequisite to achieve awakened states of consciousness and this theory is valid for all the systems present in this world. Healthy eating combined with a healthy lifestyle is critical to ensuring the successful outcome of any holistic healing system.

# Chapter Three: Tantra Techniques

While practicing tantra techniques as a couple is available in plenty, there are multiple techniques that you can use as an individual without a partner to improve your sexual, physical, and spiritual health. Here are some such techniques that you can practice alone:

## Connecting With Your Core

First, rub your palms together, so they become warm. Then, place one palm over your heart and the other palm over your genitals. Don't play or rub your chest or your genitals. Simply place your warmed palms there. Now, focus and feel the energies from these two primary energy centers radiating into your palms. Focus on this radiating energy and breathe deeply.

Imagine a circuitry that connects these two core energy centers in your body. Breathe and feel the heat transferring in the circuit between the two centers. Take a break. Again, breathe and feel the energy passing through the connected circuitry.

With sustained practice, you will be able to feel the energy flowing between these two centers more easily and more intensely than before. This energy flow is the core of your being and being aware of it will help you understand and draw from this energy.

## Squeezing Your Pelvic Muscles

In this exercise, squeeze the muscles near the place from where you pass urine in a way that mimics holding on to the desire to pee. Squeeze for a short count of up to 5 and then relax these muscles. Repeat the squeezing and relaxing processes. This technique which comes under the umbrella of Kegel exercises is referred to as pelvic floor squeeze. One squeeze and one relaxation form one set of pelvic floor squeeze exercise.

The important point to note here is that you must squeeze in such a way to understand how you feel internally rather than to hold your breath and have an external effect because of the squeeze. Again, the tightness of your squeeze is irrelevant. You must simply focus on your sensations as you squeeze and relax these muscles.

Sustained repetition every day improves the strength of these muscles and it is possible to release and use your sexual energies by performing these pelvic floor squeeze exercises.

**Tilt and Tuck**

If you have seen any pornographic films or even the usual films where the sexual act is shown, you will notice that the partners use a thrusting motion during the act wherein they move back and forth with their hips. Perhaps, many of us still use this technique even in our lives. While this may look nice for the watchers, in truth, this technique is not very pleasurable for the partners.

The better option is to bend your knees and imagine your pelvis to be a bowl (like a salad bowl) and rock it. A good analogy would be the movement of belly dancers. Try to mimic their hip movements. Start slowly and with diligent practice; you will find it easier to do the tilt and tuck motion and have more pleasure in your sexual act than with the trusting kind of motion. This tilt and tuck movement that you practice is a great way to activate the latent sexual energy at the base of your spine

## Abdominal Breathing

Most of us take breathing for granted. We simply don't understand or, rather, refuse to value its utmost importance to our lives. Except for some powerful swimmers and other sportsmen, for the average man, it is nearly impossible to remain without breathing for more than a minute. The maximum time for humans to be able to remain alive without breathing is 3 minutes. And yet, we take this divine activity for granted despite knowing that if we didn't breathe, we are dead!

So, focusing on your breath is one of the first techniques taught in any of the eastern traditions. An easy breathing technique used in tantra is abdominal breathing. Place your palm on your stomach and endeavor to breathe from there. It is very likely that breathing in this way makes you deliberately take bigger breaths than otherwise and you are bound to feel more connected to yourself too. Focusing on our breathing helps us to focus on our bodies and the movements that take place with each breath and nearly all tantra techniques are based on connecting with your body either by yourself or with your partner.

As you keep practicing, you will notice that it becomes easy to move from your headspace to your body space with just one breath.

## Practice Making Sounds

Many of us who practice masturbation feel ashamed or guilty about it and for fear of being caught in the act, we choose not to make sounds. Yes, masturbation is not really an approved sexual act in Tantra philosophy. Yet, there are times when our desire gets the better of us and we give in, right? Making articulate and sensual sounds can activate sexual energy in a much nicer way than otherwise.

Try making suitable sounds the next time and you will notice that the pleasure becomes magnified. Practice making sounds without actually masturbating or while you are doing something pleasurable such eating a succulent piece of fruit or a fabulously sweet dessert so that you can include them in your future lovemaking sessions with your partner.

## Treat Lovemaking as a Sacred Ritual

Any change first needs to take place in your mind. Shift your perspective from 'having sex' with your partner to 'making love' to your partner and performing something that will help you reach out to the divine. Set up your bedroom in the form of an altar. Put things that are special and important and connect to both of you; things that have brought both of you together, etc. Place special photos and clicks of special moments in strategic places.

Arrange sacred books that both of you enjoy reading. You can also place scared mementos like crystals and gemstones that have the power to enhance the love between the two of you; or, perhaps, help in the healing of wounds that cropped up between the two of you. Before the lovemaking session, light fragrant candles, incense, and create a wonderfully sensual and nurturing scene. Of course, it is important not to overpower the place with excessive fragrance. Use your creativity and do things that both of you can appreciate.

## Meditate Before the Lovemaking Session

Meditation before the session creates the right intent for the lovemaking. Take things gradually. First, sit in front of each other and meditate together looking into each other's eyes with love and passionate intent. In your mind, call upon your favorite deity and offer her or him your body. Visualize a ball of love and sexual energy surrounding each of you individually and one that combines this energy that envelopes both of you together.

Set intentions in place in your respective minds as to what you want to give in this lovemaking session. Talk to your partner and spell out your joint intentions. Such discussions can enhance the love and sexual energy between the two of you while creating a beautiful sense of transparency and togetherness that will only make this relationship more beautiful and stronger than before.

## Be 100% Present throughout the Session

It is important that for any relationship to nurture and get better that each partner commits herself or himself to be 100% (completely immersed) in the relationship. The same holds good even in each lovemaking session that you promise to each other. Committing ourselves to being present in the moment physically, emotionally, and spiritually has the power to take the lovemaking session to a different level where honesty, true feelings, and vulnerability also come into play.

This scenario will help both of you to delve deep into yourselves and into each other as you find new sources of sexual energy coursing through your body even before you begin the physical lovemaking session.

24

Honesty is a very important attitude to have in Tantra. Being honest about how you feel at the moment and talking about it will create a clear pathway that you can traverse to reach your partner and vice versa.

Keep checking with your body sensations and do not be in denial. For example, for women, if your yoni is not yet wet, then it means you are not ready and fully committed to receiving. It is important not to go against your natural responses and pretend to something that doesn't exist. Tell your partner you need more time, or perhaps, more foreplay.

Instead of pretensions, keep digging deep into yourself and look for blockages, resistances, and barriers that are preventing you from being 100% present there with your partner.

**Practice Tantric Massages on Each Other**

Again, take time off before the actual lovemaking session and enjoy and worship each other's body. Be fully present and conscious of every aspect of yours and your partner's body so that when the time comes, there is a perfect union. Avoid rushing into the act. Instead, continue to build up your passions because this is not mere sex but something that will help you connect with the divine. So, focus, take things slowly and enjoy every moment.

Massages are great ways to feel and enjoy each other's touch. Touching is not always a representative of erotic passion. Unbridled love can be expressed in the form of a warm hug that will set your partner's heart aflutter. However, massages done before a lovemaking session are designed to merge body and mind of the two partners.

25

The emphasis on tantric massage (or conscious touch) is on the receiver and not the giver of the massage. Both are mindfully involved in the process. Mindful massaging alights and keeps the flame of love and desire burning and burning long after the session is over. The best thing about conscious is that it is very easy and yet, unfortunately, not used by many couples. Here are a few tips:

***First, decide the basics*** – This simply means who will receive and who will give. You could take turns to do the receiving and giving. However, it is not possible to receive and give simultaneously with full awareness because it is easy to get lost between the two. The receiver will sit or lie down in a comfortable position with eyes closed. The giver should find a convenient position to place himself or herself conveniently close to the receiver.

***Synchronize your breathing*** – Breathing together is a critical aspect of connected lovemaking. Synchronize your breathing by observing the receiver's breathing. It is usually the giver who matches his or her breathing to that of the receiver. This is a way of telling the receiver that you as a giver are holding the space for him or her. This step is bound to take some time as both the partners will have to get into their natural breathing rhythm and yet, find the way to synchronize with the other and relax in the entire process.

***Be aware of how you are feeling*** – Focus on your own feeling and be totally aware of the state of mind you are in at that point in time. Do not judge your feelings or your body sensations. Simply observe the feeling. This should be done by both the receiver and giver. When you are acutely aware of yourself at any moment in time, it is easy to pass on this sense of mindfulness and awareness to your partner as well. When both the partners do it in harmony, there is bound to be sensations that resonate with each other.

***Make sure your intent to give reflects in your touch*** – the True intention is the biggest motivation to get things done in an intended way. When you are massaging, make sure your intention to give unconditionally is reflected in your touch. The receiver could make a request as to where and how he or she wants the touch to take place. The giver should then put his or her full intent to giving what the receiver requested.

***Literally, touch from your heart*** – Start the touch connection from your heart, literally. Ideally, the giver should place his or her hand over the receiver's heart by first placing the palm followed by the fingers. This position will ensure that the hearts of the receiver and the giver are directly connected through the left arm of the giver. This position literally connects the partners at their hearts.

Again, check if your breathing is synchronized and for a moment, feel the heart of your receiving partner beating on your palm. Now, place the right hand at the point where the massage needs to be given. Again, place the palm first so that there is stability in the hold. At this point, the receivers must mindfully feel the palm of the giver on the agreed body position and open his or her heart to receive the conscious touch. Stay connected like this for as long as you want and feel your hearts connected. This can be a very humbling moment as heart-to-heart connects have the power to create humility in a relationship.

***Enjoy the massaging mindfully and together*** –
Now, slowly move your hands through the receiver's
body while being mindfully aware that your breath and
your palms on your hearts are grounding both of you.
Ask the receiver to 'actively' enjoy the massage through
use of gentle sighs and pleasurable sounds. This will
help the receiver to be mindfully aware of the giver's
touch instead of allowing his or her mind to go off on
its own path. Givers should follow their instincts for the
right kind of pressure and direction to take in the
massaging process. There could be added connection if
eye contact can be maintained between the giver and
the receiver.

***Finally, trust your ability to give and receive
love*** – Trust your body's ability to give and receive
pleasure and by doing this, you are facilitating a deeper
communicative connection with your partner that goes
beyond words. Avoid worrying about doing things
right. Instead, trust your instincts and create deep
erotic connections with your lover.

## Tantric Third-Eye Meditation Technique

Tantric practices include the use of breath, movement,
sound, and meditation in order to open the energy
channels in the chakra system and allow the released
energy to flow from the base roots upward to reach the
crown chakra. Meditation is a technique that is
followed vigorously in tantric practices. The following
extremely simple meditation technique can be singly or
before a lovemaking session with the two partners
sitting in front of each other.

The Third-Eye meditation also referred to as a Spinal
Meditation, helps in opening the Crown and the Third

Eye Chakras to receive divine powers from the Universe. It also facilitates the energy flow up and down the spinal cord which helps in enhancing the awareness of the Universe and its limitless powers. Moreover, this meditation also helps you remain grounded as well.

Sit comfortably either cross-legged on the floor or in a chair. If you are sitting cross-legged on the floor, feel the pressure of your bones at the base of the pelvis as it meets the cushion or floor. If you are sitting in a chair, let your feet feel the coldness of the ground.

Now, breathe in and lengthen your spinal cord in such a way like as if someone has tied a string to your spine and is pulling it in the upward direction. Then, breathe out in such a way that your tailbone is appearing to reach the floor with the length of the spine being maintained same as before. Imagine your tailbone to work like a tap root that is affixed to the earth holding a tree or plant up erect. Keep your breathing in and out at a natural pace.

Now, put the tip of your tongue on the roof of your mouth and imagine a round golden ball at the third eye chakra location (between your brows on your forehead). While inhaling through your nose, roll the golden ball to touch the Crown chakra and then let it slide down the spine right up to the tailbone. During this time, you must chant the mantra, 'hung.'

When you exhale, toss the ball upward from your tailbone and let it travel through the spine until it reaches the third eye location after touching the Crown chakra. During the upward movement of the golden ball, you must chant the mantra, 'sau' (rhyming with 'saw').

This chant translates to 'I am' or 'I am that' which means this body, mind, and spirit are part of the universal consciousness. Therefore, chanting of this mantra reaffirms your true self as being one with the Earth (rooted through the tailbone) and the Divine (which is connected via the imaginary string attached to the top of the spine). Begin this practice by doing for 5 minutes daily. Slowly, increase your duration at regular intervals until you build it up to 20 minutes every day.

Any activity that activates the energy flow in your body must necessarily be balanced by a grounding activity that keeps you rooted and stabilized. While activated chakras are great to experience higher levels of consciousness, an ever-activated energy system can be very difficult to handle at the earthly plane and to counter this, balancing and rooting activities will help you keep energy activation in check and facilitate grounding.

So, in effect, by practicing this tantric meditation, you will have access to the higher powers of this world while remaining grounded so as to leverage those powers to lead a happier and more fulfilled life than before. Practice the third-eye meditation alone first. When you are sufficiently comfortable with it, you can do this meditation technique with your partner sitting opposite each other to get into the zone of lovemaking.

# Chapter Four: Yantras and Mantras

In addition to breathing and other techniques used in tantra practices, yantras and mantras are also commonly included. This chapter deals with Yantras and some of the mantras used in Tantra.

## What are Yantras?

Yantra, in its literal translation from Sanskrit, means 'instrument' or a 'support.' In tantra practice, a Yantra is usually a geometrical design that is employed as a very effective tool to support the practitioner in meditative, contemplative, and concentration activities. Yantras represent the macrocosm in a microcosmic frame and acts like a gateway to and from the higher planes of consciousness. Yantras are all spiritually significant designs and every aspect has specific meanings pertaining to the higher planes of consciousness.

The Yantra in tantric practices behaves like a window to the universal divine being or the absolute one, as this power is many times referred to. When you compel your mind to focus on a single design or object (the yantra in this case), the overwhelming mental chatter that clutters your mind is reduced. With practice, it is possible to completely eliminate mindless chatter in your mind. When the mind has achieved calmness and complete stillness, the yantra is dropped by the practitioners. A seasoned tantric practitioner only needs to visualize the yantra in his mind to reach the calm state of mind.

Yantras are usually designed symmetrically in such a way that the practitioner's eyes can be focused on the center. Yantras can be drawn on paper, on wood, on metal, or directly on the earth. They can also be three-dimensional objects. In India, the most famous one is the Sri Vidya yantra that represents the deity Tripura Sundari. This symbol is a microcosm of the entire universe and is used to remind the practitioners that there is no difference between the object and the subject.

**Operation of Yantras**

'Form energy' of 'shape energy' or the concept that every form or shape emits a particular energy pattern and frequency, is the basis of the operation of any yantra. Examples of such yantras that are seen even in Judaism and Christianity include the 5-pointed star or the Pentagon, the Star of David, the pyramids, the Cross, etc. These shapes are given different degrees of negative and positive power (or evil and/or good power). In Tantra practices, only those shapes that have positive attributes and those with harmonious and beneficial energies are used.

When a practitioner focuses on the particular yantra, his or her mind automatically tunes in to the 'resonating' frequency or energy pattern of that yantra. Continued focus helps in maintaining and amplifying this resonating effect. It is important to remember at this point that the energy itself as a result of the focusing exercise comes from the macrocosm and not from the yantra.

Therefore, yantras are instruments or tools that help us achieve resonance with a particular frequency from the macrocosm. The yantra facilitates the practitioner to 'tune in' to the desired frequency from the macrocosm.

It is possible to effectively use yantras to put the practitioner into elevated energy levels in the universe.

## Types of Yantras Used in Tantric Practices

Unfortunately, the Western world is yet to understand the true meaning and the resonating power of a yantra. Many dubious tantric schools claim that they can draw Yantras by drawing on their imagination. This is not true. Every mood and every emotion has a specific yantra associated with it through the energy that its form and shape represents.

The traditional Yantras were not drawn from imagination but revealed through divine design and through clairvoyance. Revealing a new yantra to the world requires the limitless tantric powers of a true guru and taking all and sundry 'designs' available on the internet as a yantra will only reduce the power and influence of your tantric practice.

Yantras and mantras are connected in the sense that a particular yantra needs to be focused on by chanting a corresponding mantra. Here are a few yantras along with a basic understanding of each of their resonance.

***The Dot or the Bindu*** – The Bindu represented focalized energy brought on by intense concentration. It can be seen as a deposit or reservoir of concentrated energy. In Tantric practice, the dot is considered to represent Siva Himself, the masculine source of all creation.

***The Triangle or the Trikona*** – This is a symbol of Shakti, the feminine source of all creation. A downward pointing triangle represents the female sexual organ, the yoni, the Universe's supreme source. An upward pointing triangle represents the supreme spiritual aspiration of being one with the absolute. Also, the downward triangle represents water which tends to flow down while the upward triangle represents fire which goes UP always.

**The 6-Pointed Star of the Shatkona** – Two triangles, one upward-facing, and the other downward facing, superimposed over each other combine to form the shatkona, referred to as David's star in Judaism. This symbol represents the union of Siva and Shakti, without which there can be NO creation.

**The Circle or the Chakra** – Representing rotation, the circle is another commonly used symbol either by itself or as part of a more complex yantra in tantric practices. Rotation is also a movement that is very closely connected with spiraling movement, the basis of the evolution in the macrocosm. Moreover, the chakra or the circle is also a represented of the creative void and perfection. It symbolizes the wind element of nature.

**The Lotus Symbol** – This is a symbol of variety (each petal representing something different) and purity owing to the flower's ability to rise above a dirty pond to remain beautiful and pure.

**The Square or the Bhupura** – Representing the element earth, the square symbol is normally the external contour of a yantra. Usually, a yantra uses the square as the contour and the dot as the center. The reason for this is the concept in tantra that the universe starts from the subtle (the dot – concentrated energy) and moves toward the gross (or the earth and life systems).

Many of the complex yantras also include other symbols such as arrows, swords, tridents, etc. representing the direction and purpose of action of the form energy the yantra signifies.

## How to Use Yantras in Tantric Practices

As already explained, resonance is the critical aspect of any yantra. The resonating effect of the yantra can be initiated and maintained by focusing on its image. The mind should be tuned to the resonating energy of the particular yantra for activation and sustenance of energy flow. Here are some instructions on the correct use of yantras:

Hang the Yantra on any wall facing East or North ensuring the center of the image is in line with your eyes.

When meditating, sit in a comfortable position that you are accustomed to.

Inhale through the nose and exhale through your mouth in your natural breathing rhythm without trying to control your breath.

Focus on the center of the yantra with as little blinking as possible. Keep the focus of your eyes on the center and watch the entire yantra as one.

You can start with 5 minutes each day of this meditating exercise and then, slowly increase the duration until you can do about half an hour a day.

It is recommended that you aspire to achieve the levels of resonating energy that the yantra is capable of delivering and your aspiration is bound to be fulfilled sooner than later.

Seasoned tantric practitioners can reach such amazing depths in their focus that it is difficult for them to tell whether the yantra is within them or whether they are inside the yantra.

## Importance of Mantra in Tantric Practices

Chanting and practicing mantras in tantra is designed to help you achieve the dhyana state which translates to contemplate or to imagine. Meditation through mantra is not being 'lost' in thought. Instead, it an active state of mind where deep awareness can be experienced is a seamless flow of thoughts. When you achieve this meditative state, your consciousness is expanded such that space represented by Shakti unites with time represented by Siva resulting in a cosmic union, the microcosm of which is believed in tantra to be the sexual union between man and woman on earth.

Mantras are connected with the human aspect through the deity they represent or signify. Deities, in tantra practice, are also functional manifestations of the universal absolute of which we are all apart. Deities are manifested internally and externally through the human body and can be accessed by experience and/or cognition. Mantras connect the human to the particular deity. In short, mantras are a sacred formula in the form of vibrations and sounds that represent the associated deity which is a function of the entire universe.

Here are a few mantras associated with the respective deity along with the results of chanting them consistently:

## Deity – Mantra – Results

Ganesha – Gam – success and protection
Kali – Krim – victory, protection, and liberation
Lakshmi – Shrim – beauty, prosperity, and wealth
Saraswati – Aim – Knowledge, arts, music, and sensibility
Shiva – Om Namah Shivaya or Hum – awareness, protection, and liberation
Shakti – Hrim – family, energy, and good moral qualities

## How to Practice Mantra

When you practice mantra persistently, your mind is getting closer and closer to the vibration and sound of the mantra thereby creating a link between you and the particular deity. You should sit comfortably and recite the mantra at the same speed as your natural speech. Do not try to hurry the repetition of the mantra. Even as thoughts come and go in your mind, you must persist in pronouncing or mouthing the mantra with as little distractions as possible. You can also combine this with meditating with your yantra and focus on it while you recite your mantra.

Depending on your desired results, you can choose to change the mantra. For the desires of knowledge, use the Saraswati mantra, if you desire wealth, use the Lakshmi mantra, etc. Using mantras are a great way of bringing in your meditative powers while helping you connect with a more powerful function of the universal energy than your own.

# Chapter Five: Asanas in Tantra

The final chapter will talk about the most intimate thing of Tantric practices and that is a sexual union in order to achieve divine revelation while enhancing the love and passion in any relationship. This chapter talks about the various asanas used in tantric practice.

Whether we know it or not, love is the ultimate law of nature and everything revolves around this amazing element. Tantra yoga has been passed down by the wise sages to help couples transmit this love between themselves so that there is harmony, joy, and passion in their relationship. The asanas mentioned here can be performed anytime, but if done before lovemaking session can empower the sexual union to help achieve supreme bliss for both partners.

## Navasana or the Ship's Pose

This asana is designed to specifically enhance trust between partners and let the love between the two of you become a dependable element in both your lives. Sit in front of each other and keeping your knees bent, let your soles touch those of your partner's. Hold hands. If you cannot reach each other's hands, then take the help of a scarf to hold each end.

Now, keep your spine as straight as possible and lift both your feet with your soles still in contact with each other. Start with one set of foot and then move on to the next. Once, you have both your soul-touching feet (like palms joined together) straight above, try and keep your chest and spine as erect as you possibly can. Hold the ship pose as long as both of you can without overly straining any part of your body.

## Virabhadrasana or the Hero's Pose

This asana is meant to increase the feeling of spiritual love in both of you. When you practice this pose with persistence, you will notice that as a couple you are able to overcome obstacles in a smoother and easier way than before. You will find enhanced energy levels in your body and mind helping you achieve your combined goals.

This asana has to be performed both in the right and the left sides. For the left side, here is what you do.

Face your partner and put your right foot forward. Both of you must do this resulting in your right feet touching each other along the shank on the inner side. Now, lift your arms and bring the palms forward facing each other so that your right palm is in full contact with the right palm of your lover and the left palms are also touching the same way. Press the palms tightly together.

Now, put your left foot back as if you are taking a huge step with the ankle making a 45-degree angle with the ground. Keep the soles of both your feet firmly on the ground. The right knee should be bent so as to form a right angle. Breathe calmly and look with passion into your partner's eyes. Come out of this asana slowly and deliberately pulling back each part of your hands and legs to their normal positions. Now, do the same on the right side which will entail you to put your left foot forward and your right foot back.

## The V Letter

This asana is meant to take your trust and intimacy to even further levels. Holding on to each other's wrists, bend as much backward as you can with the trust that your partner will not let go of your wrists and that you will not let go of your partner's wrists. This pose will ideally result in the letter V being formed by your two bodies.

Focus on the flow of energy between yourselves through the connected arms. The more you resonate with each other's energy, the more you will find it easy to balance the other in the pose. Continued practice will help in improving the ability of both partners to resonate with the energy of the other partner and this will build enhanced trust and intimacy between the two of you.

**Vrikshasana or the Tree Pose**

The pose is designed to help couples increase their capability to view and achieve higher goals and ideals in their combined lives. The two partners will be able to achieve higher planes of consciousness by acceding to each other's high ideals.

Stand next to each other with a little bit of gap between the two of you. Place the arm that is closest to your partner around his or her waist. So, here, one partner will have the left arm around the other partner's waist and the latter will have the right arm around the former's waist.

Now, lift the leg that is farther away from your partner and bend the knee and bring the foot forward to touch the inner respective thigh. Next, bring the arm that is away from the partner over your respective head and touch your partner's palm so as to fully be in contact. Come out of the asana slowly and deliberately. Repeat on the other side so that the left and right sides of both partners are equally used.

## The Bicycle Pose

Lie on your backs with the knees bent and facing each other. Now, bend your knees and take it up to your chest and let your partner do the same ensuring that the soles of your feet are in contact fully. Place the weight of your body on your lower backs. Keep your hands away as they are not needed for this asana. Intertwining the fingers and placing them under your neck would be a comfortable position for your hands. So, now both of you are on your backs with the knees close to or touching your chest and the soles of your feet in full contact.

Breathe for a while and once you get your rhythm with your partner, start the pedaling action with the soles still in touch. As you change the leg which is pedaling, you can shift your torso appropriately keeping your abdominal muscles as stiff as possible. Breathe in through your nose and breathe out through your mouth, each time the torso needs to be shifted during the pedaling action. You will feel a wonderful sense of dynamism and joy pervading both of you and the effervescence will be unmistakable. Come out of the asana slowly.

## Ustrasana or the Camel Pose

This asana facilitates the couple to achieve a sense of euphoria combined with empathy as both of your inner willpower harmonizes with each other. Kneel and face your partner as he or she does the same thing facing toward you. Now, holding each other's elbow, bend backward without putting stress on your neck muscles.

Ensure your knee is kept at a 90-degree angle. Feel the energies flowing between your bodies through the connecting arms.

If you notice, each of these poses can also be done alone, individually. So, do them individually until each of you has achieved perfection in the asanas. Then, as per tantric practices, combine the yoga performance and do them as a couple. Here are some amazing benefits of performing yoga together as a couple, especially before lovemaking sessions:

- It helps in creating a genuine and deep connection between the couples and these deep bonds help you go beyond customary ties and with practice can help you achieve union at a much higher consciousness than the human level.

- It can deepen and enhance your spiritual, physical, psychic, erotic, and mental connections with each other in unimaginable ways.

- Performing yoga as a couple has the power to bring in harmony, beauty, refinement, and sheer strength to the relationship.

- Your relationship will be able to reflect each other's deepest secrets and desires that were hitherto obscure to both of you. Couple yoga helps you manifest your deepest desire to your partner and vice versa and that too, without fear of embarrassment, being judged, or anything else that forms the basest aspect of humankind.

- A beautiful relationship borne out of doing couple yoga can not only help in uplifting your own souls but also help in improving the interactions and relationships of other people in and around your personal and professional life.

- In addition to yoga, if the partners indulge in sexual continence, then the ensuing release of energy will cover a wider sphere of people. Just like how a little candle can radiate light in any dark room, similarly, true love can radiate happiness unconditionally everywhere.

# Chapter Six: Tantric Sexual Techniques

Now, that you understand why tantra uses the sexual union as the way to achieve divine enlightenment; let us look as at some of the sexual techniques proposed by tantric sex positions that will help you achieve happiness along with supreme sexual pleasure, many times with continence too. So, here goes.

Before you get into the actual act, the following tips will ensure your sexual encounters are fulfilling and deeply satisfying for both of you:

*Choose a convenient day* – Tantric sex does not involve a 10-12 minute thrust in-thrust out technique. It is slow and sensual and takes time. Choose a day that is convenient to both partners and ensures that there is a commitment of 2 hours to the entire exercise. Once, the time is fixed and committed by both partners; it is important to feel disciplined and not put off the scheduled event. Even if you are tired, get started, and watch your fatigue melt into nothingness as you experience rejuvenating love.

*Be open to try new and novel techniques* – For successful tantric sex practices, it is very important to keep an open heart and open mind. The act is not relegated to some form of cheap sex. It is divine and an act that has the power to energize and change the perspective of the partners towards who they are and what the world is. For this, you must be ready and open to trying new and novel things that you have not tried before. Free yourself from conditioned shackles.

*Set the right mood* – Light scented candles or incense and make the room sensual and nice. It would help if you can have a refreshing, scented bath as well.

Give each other compliments by telling what you like in the other. Do not hesitate to look deeply into each other's eyes and try to see beyond what the eyes seem to show you. Delve deep and find that connection between the two of you.

*Meditate together* – Using some of the techniques listed in this book, meditate together by sitting in front of each other. Looking at each other's bodies without actually touching can be a highly pleasurable experience and also will help you understand each other's strengths and weaknesses.

You could simply sit and breathe deeply and attempt to synchronize your breaths. With practice, you can include yantras and mantras to enhance the feeling of togetherness as you meditate and feel each other's spiritual, emotional, and physical presence more acutely than before.

*Perform a few couple yoga asanas* – Considering the immense benefits of performing yoga together; it makes a lot of sense to do a couple of asanas together and get even closer to each other physically and spiritually than before.

*Get intimate with each other by sitting in the Yab-Yum pose* – The Yab-Yum pose has been designed to enhance intimacy between the partners in some amazingly unimaginable ways. Sitting in this position, your souls and hearts can merge together to achieve supreme bliss. The man has to sit cross-legged on the floor or on the bed. The woman has to sit on her man's lap. Let her wrap her legs around his waist and her arms around his neck. The pose can be performed either with clothes on or in the naked form. The choice is entirely both of yours make.

In this position, embrace each other deeply and try and synchronize your breathing again. Allow your bodies to feel and tune in to each other and feel your heart and soul merging in this beautiful and loving embrace that can be devoid of all sexual feeling but totally filled with feelings of love, joy, and togetherness.

Hold on for as long as you want to feel each other's love, breath, and happiness. It can be a very special moment for both partners. This pose is excellent to celebrate your unique and beautiful relationship. You can kiss in this position to feel the love even deeper.

***Give each other a good massage*** – Again, taking the tips and ideas given in this book, take turns to be the giver and receiver of the massage and enjoy each other's touch. You can start from non-erotic positions like the neck, back, arms, etc., and slowly and gradually, move your fingers and hands to do their magic right through all parts of receiver's body. Do not forget to take and receive feedback so that the receiver remains in the joy of the massage instead of letting his or her thoughts fly somewhere else.

Now, let us look at some basic tantric sex positions for you to try tonight itself:

## Position 1

The male partner should kneel behind the female while tilting slightly backward. The female should have her back to the male and should also kneel down with legs tucked between his legs. Now, both of your sit down on your calves and thighs ensuring your bodies are tightly squeezed together.

Let the male partner wrap his arms around the female partner's waist holding her tightly to his body. Now, let his penis get inside you and once he is inside, do the tilt and tuck movement together. You can also do circular movements together. When you are tired, take breaks by simply sitting in the same position holding your bodies tightly squeezed together.

As the male partner is tilting slightly backward, he will be able to reach the female's G-spot which is, perhaps, one of the most pleasurable spots for a woman. Moreover, as the female's butt is tightly squeezed to his thighs, his groin will fit snugly inside you enhancing the pleasure for both of you.

## Position 2

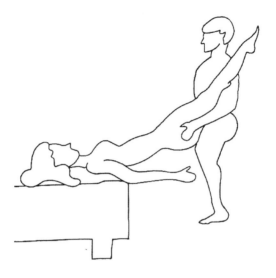

Let the female partner lie on her back at the edge of the bed, tabletop, or any other countertop with a pillow under her back for a bit of elevation. She must extend her legs in the upward direction so that her opening is right at the edge of the bed or table. Keeping the legs straight up will be very beneficial for the entire act. She can use her hands to keep her legs raised higher so that her pelvis is also raised.

Now, the male partner can enter the female while standing or kneeling down if the table is very low. Holding the female straightened legs will give him leverage while helping the female get balance too. He can now thrust inside with added stability for both the

49

partners. It is important to keep the female legs as much as possible together.

Keeping the legs close together gives you a very tight fit ensuring there is sufficient and blissful friction during the tilt and tuck motion of the lovemaking session. Loosening the female legs and getting them back tightly together will give added pleasure to both of the partners.

## Position 3

Let the woman stand at the edge of the bed or couch with feet and legs wide apart. The man will stand on the floor with the feet firmly on the ground very close to his woman, facing her. Adjusting the width of the woman's stance, the man can find the right position to get inside her so that both their pelvises touch each other. Now, do the tilt and tuck motion together to feel the supreme bliss of being inside each other.

The stability of this pose enhances pleasure for both of you without worrying about the stress on any body part. Moreover, legs wide apart make the woman feel vulnerable which only enhances the love of the man for his woman. The continuous friction on the front side is sure to hit the g-spot of the woman which, enhances her pleasure to great heights.

As both the partners are standing, there is very little to hold back. The hands will be free to do other erotic activities on each other's bodies resulting in added pleasure during the entire process.

When both are satiated and happy with the entire ritual, you can indulge in the yab-yum pose again before giving up these wonderful moments of togetherness. The energy release during a tantric sex ritual does not enervate. It invigorates you and your partner to take and receive more from each other and the universe, at large. Remember to give 100% of yourselves to the other partner.

# Conclusion

One of the primary principles of Tantra is there is no form of energy in the Universe that does not exist in our body. Tantra also means technique and it is that which helps us leverage the different forms of energy available in our body in a conscious way so that there is increased productivity in your life.

Although the secrets of the Tantra tradition was kept a secret for hundreds of years for multiple reasons including the chances of them being misunderstood and misinterpreted, today, thanks to the internet and the world becoming a global village, more and more people are clearing their heads of misunderstandings and are given themselves to the magic of this system to lead a more fulfilled, happy, and healthy lifestyle than before.

Tantric traditions and their rituals are designed to draw out the subtle energies in our body and work with them to alleviate the practitioner both physically and spiritually. Tantric practices empower you to explore and leverage the power within you while eliminating physical and mental blocks that prevent you from achieving your best.

Remember that we are all born as Tantric lovers because we are all part of the ultimate divine. We are the pure presence if only we could find the power and wherewithal to tear away the layers that have been laid on this pure essence through years of mistaken conditioning. Again, sex is definitely a part of tantric practices; but tantra sex is founded on pure love that is the basis of the pure essence drawn from the omnipresent divine.

Tantra practices are designed to help you connect with yourself, with your partner, and with the divine. Tantra is a potent combination of spirituality and sexuality to help us understand ourselves better thereby empowering us to lead more fulfilling, contented, and lives, irrespective of our social standing, our gender, our caste, our race, our nationality, or anything else.

Living a life based on Tantric practices helps us achieve balance through the integration of feminine and masculine aspects of ourselves so that we feel a sense of wholesome that is presently lacking in our lives. Tantric practices help us see the divine in everything around us. These practices (if done patiently and diligently) infuse our senses and bodies with copious amounts of unbridled and unconditional love and compassion for one and all.

Additionally, when we practice Tantra, we are rid of baseless shame, guilt, and embarrassment associated with our sexuality that are again built around insensitive conditioning of our society. So, bringing in Tantra into your life translates to more love, compassion, and an increased sense or perception of the divine.

Tantric practices also help you use the preserved energy to find your true purpose. Of course, it is important to start small, begin with the simple individual and couple techniques mentioned in this book (which can be started immediately) and once you have mastered the simple ones and drawn the amazing benefits of even these simple tantric practices, you can move on and learn more advanced techniques from reputable teachers and take your life to an entirely new level of consciousness.

One last thing. We would be super happy if you took the time to give us some feedback so we can improve the book. You can do that by posting a review on the Amazon product page. Thank you very much in advance!

Resources

https://medium.com/@matthiasrose/the-origins-of-tantra-acc4334638e9
https://psiloveyou.xyz/tantra-shmantra-d52c6a35923d
http://www.oztantra.com/tantric-history-2/
http://www.yogamag.net/archives/1981/joct81/womrole.shtml
https://www.healthcentral.com/article/the-spiritual-and-health-benefits-of-tantra-yoga
http://www.stylecraze.com/articles/tantric-yoga-benefits/#gref
http://www.anamayaresort.com/tantra-yoga-benefits/
https://www.mindbodygreen.com/0-17370/a-tantra-meditation-to-enhance-your-love-life.html
https://www.mindbodygreen.com/0-17733/6-practices-to-awaken-the-tantric-lover-within.html
https://www.elephantjournal.com/2017/08/5-ways-to-begin-practicing-tantra/
http://www.sivasakti.com/tantra/introduction-to-yantra/
http://www.spirit-web.org/yoga/tantra-yoga/the-practice-of-tantric-mantras
http://www.allabouttantra.info/en/english/52-couple-asanas
http://www.cosmopolitan.com/tantric-sex-positions/
https://mytinysecrets.com/tantra-101-a-super-simple-guide-for-tantric-sex-beginners/

Printed in the USA
CPSIA information can be obtained
at www.ICGtesting.com
LVHW010826260124
769834LV00001B/136

9 789198 630886